Tips for Teaching in America

Poems by Joshua Roark

Special SXSW 2026 Edition

Unsolicited Press
Portland, Oregon
www.unsolicitedpress.com
info@unsolicitedpress.com
619–354–8005

TIPS FOR TEACHING IN AMERICA

ISBN: 978-1-969421-98-3

Distributed by Asterism Books
https://asterismbooks.com/

For wholesale orders:
Asterism Books
568 1st Avenue South, Ste 120
Seattle, WA 98104
(206) 485-4829
info@asterismbooks.com

Cover Design: Chelsea Wales D'Errico
Editor: Summer Stewart

Author's Note

Dear Reader,

When Jack reads from *Tips for Teaching in America* in the film, he's holding the first edition of this little book.

I am thrilled to share this new edition in celebration of the premiere of *Dead Deer High* at SXSW.

These poems were originally written and published years before the film, and whenever I reread them, I am thrust full-hearted into my time teaching 8th graders in the Mississippi Delta. Stephanie, Kyle, JT, and Vok would not exist without them.

Like the film, I hope it brings you joy and helps connect you with the poets and teachers in your lives.

Sincerely,
Joshua Roark

You can find more info about the film by scanning the QR code or visiting deaddeerhigh.com.

Please sign up for the newsletter to stay up to date on how you can watch and share the film.

All inquiries are welcome to deaddeerhigh@gmail.com, or our publicist Jason Kaspersky at jk@prodigypublicrelations.com.

Contents

Tips for Teaching in America

(C) Antibodies

Bodies, thirty-four human bodies
Cleaved into standard sized
Bubbles, scantron creatures

Benched in a row, you'd think
All the cafeteria were
Deserted but for the sticky

Clicks of hand-me-down calculators
And the jerky whisper of pages
Curling over—but if you

Could hear eyes roll or spirits
Break there'd be a rock
Concert in here like

At the usual lunching hour
After you measure out noon to noon-thirty
By the bite marks on pizza

Cubes, gray and flat like candles, *three*
Bites to go until we walk in
Circles outside—now though you

1

Can only measure out time
By the heads-in-elbows
As you stalk, arms folded,

Between the tables
As usual, stiff-backed
Dignity slipping

Away as usual, watching little
Dots get scribbled in for the
Alphabet of every name

And every number of every state-
Documented name until
All that they say matters

Can fit on a stocky half sheet
Colored like dirt and spotted
All over like something sick and

Dying, maybe infectious

Buy Your Own Classroom Supplies

Your classroom binder should be big, beefy,
yellow maybe, or red, easy for spotting,
smudged with something like chocolate, coffee
splashed across the pages and set in the rings.

Your pens should be sunset colored, show that
you mean business, even from your pocket
or dry, chapped hands—oh, and don't forget
the bottle of sanitizer. It'll sit fat

like a trophy at the edge of your desk.
Your closet should hold four white button-up
shirts, two pairs of heavy polyester
pants, black, creased, and a single ink-black clip-
on-tie, bought at an army surplus store.
Trust me, full length ties are not worth the risk.

Not all of them, but some in the classroom laugh,
fleshy bubbles of noise that slow rise up
in front of your words, cutting instructions in half.
You smile and sigh and take your cue to shut-up.

Pencil ends wiggle in their growing grips
like the tails of so many happy dogs.
Just write, you tell them, you know their tricks,
Let honesty spring from that young mind s fog.

Some do scribble honestly on the page,
their hands dancing a quick beat of hurt and play
to create, to dig, to lift and reach and rage
toward the graphite honesty they struggle to say.

Why s it gotta be honest? she asks through gum.
You shrug, she shrugs. They write. Not all, but some.

Keep a Few Dollars in Your Desk

Three teenagers die at the road's little
bridge on old 82, a few miles out.
Concrete knocked down river swallowed, metal
bent back. The kids ask you when, why and how
and the tough girl with scars and hollow laughs
says she was cousined to one of the teens,
could you help to get balloons from dollar shack?
So they can be let loose and whole-town-seen?

Bus driver preacher—worn Bible in hand,
orange bus at back—expounds on texting,
as the purple balloons ascend up high,
so blue and bare to all their upgazed eyes.
To the sky the young necks have already bent,
the highway's silence too loud to listen.

5

They Teach You to Repeat Directions

Feet flat. Backs straight. Eyes up.
Their eyes: jewels pried from a stolen crown
and buried deep in the Mississippi Delta.
Like the arrowheads you dug up with your grandpa
Feet flat. Backs straight. Eyes up.
out in the corn field where he'd take you shooting,
blades of black ice, crooked in the hollow
cup of your palm, once sacred in the light.
Feet flat. Backs straight. Eyes up.
They have the eyes that all children have,
then give up in dark procedure
Feet flat. Backs straight. Eyes up.
to life, to each other, and to the classroom walls,
cement brick and off-white.
       Eyes up.

Cover Your Door with Student Art

Darkness hangs low in the half-light
from the window and the lamp, and the classroom hum
breaks on the whisper of pages turning from the right
to the left, that unconscious two-step of thumbs.

Something pleasant happens when they're all reading.
A quiet drifts lazily from chair to chair,
reaches down to hold their hands, leading
us from word to word in classroom prayer.

Then a suit peers through the slim window on the door
and all of it shrinks, the air stale-turned,
the young bodies now shifting in their seats, bored,
asking just what exactly they're supposed to learn.

The easy letting go of our thoughts is lost;
our minds forget the steps to that wordy waltz.

Principals Were Once Teachers Too

Observation Notes (May 16th):
Curriculum Objectives are not legibly written
on the dry-erase board in black marker.
Teacher stares out the window too much,
makes him look weak and uncertain.
Students giggling during Independent
Reading time, teacher in his book, too engrossed.
Student poetry is not in the District Plan,
bad (*slang* does not rhyme with *fame*).
The Wall of Shame has not been updated
in four days, inflated data reports.
Quiet students resort to requesting
to work outside, suggesting weak command.
Room has too many antique lamps.

There's a Classroom Feeling

On the bare skin of the nerdy girl's knees
as she sits half-slouched half-bent
half-tense in the plastic scoop of her desk,
sneakers tucked carefully beneath herself.
The heater's broken today, cold and cloudy,
and everyone is wearing sweaters or hoodies
or their big sister's old pink jacket as they read,
so the feeling just meanders from chair to chair.
You can half-glimpse it standing tip-toe,
nestling into one boy's tight brown curls,
then holding still, playful, like a dancer leaning
at the edge of a stage. The boy shifts his weight
and you look away just as the feeling settles
like a firm dark weight on the flat of your stomach.

Like a firm dark weight on the flat of your stomach
the weariness pushes you gently into your chair.
Rowed stalks of corn out the window glint
like a thousand rusty knives for a moment,
caught by a slant of sun leaning down.
The weariness must've snuck across the room
to the oldest boy, tickled his nose, because he snores
from under his gray hoodie, or fake snores,
a long *hngGGghh-Pphhaaaww,*

and all of us let loose spools of laughter
to fill the room—eyeing each other for approval—
louder than called for really, louder and louder,
until some fool starts jumping in their chair,
scraping the bare skin of the nerdy girl's knee.

The train tracks are quiet and modest;

they don't like to talk about themselves.

I don't judge y'all, nope, not me.

If God wants you two together, His will!

Other people judge, sure, but not me.

Y'all are fine by me. Really.

Part B. Select the two pieces of evidence

that best support your answer from Part A:

The train tracks can make things straight if

chin and navel rest on the long cool metal.

Oh we have a special visitor today!

Come on in, Welcome to our Church!

Thank you so much for coming today!

Me and my cousin went trick-or-treating

on the white folks side this year!

The train tracks divide north from black;

the train tracks divide white from south.

My dad thought I was crazy to do it.

I just went up to her and started talking to her!

Why do all the dogs bark at me and not you?

Once a year, the tracks still grow white

beards of cotton from what the trains throw off.

Part A. Which sentence should be included

in an ***objective*** summary of this passage?

I heard those kids can be real tough to handle.
God bless you folks for coming in.
Is it hell over there? Those kids can be real trouble.
They have such hard lives, you know?

Don't Trust the Dictionary You Came With

You need to talk about Michael Brown's body,
lying in the street like forgotten luggage
from noon to four p.m. Debate the cop's
language, TV's language, #language.
Then talk about Eric Gardner's body.
Was he a crazed "demon" too? Was his language
merely meant for those three last words? *Street" is a
synonym for bed,* says the girl with the knot
of red braids, *and Gurley died in the stairs, so safe"*
now means nowhere, and their heads all nod
through the room, chins on hidden strings, their mouths
whispering the other names, renaming the truth:
Trayvon, Cameron, Laquan, and Tamir too,
what did language class ever do for you?

Teach Grammar Through Multi-Media

—the street where the rules finally
make sense by counting the shoes that lie
in clumps like commas edited from the street
to be seen is all the they re asking for Phil
squints at the scene now punctuated by
black bandanas and megaphones crying
out *pour bodies like water from the homes*
at the sound of *Water! Milk! Water!* fills the
the classroom till the speakers cut out for
a moment this country will always—wait
that was the sound of gunfire starting up
again *the street is filled with all these people*
coughing and crying Phil just all these folks
retching sounds from bodies flat against—

Bridge Cultures During Planning Period

Your left hand settles on
that usual place above
your hip, elbow cocked out.

I didn t know all this,
Mrs. A--- from Pakistan
teaches SPED, her body
folded into a desk,
They should come out with it!

Late August news plays on
the screen, lights the off-white
brick walls with waves of blue
and red—*I didn t know!*

And you nod too—*I didn t
know*—your face red and blue.

Determine the Meaning of Words and Phrases

Part A. Read the passage below.

Benderrious calls you over and says, Look, this world is like ours, too." He points to a line about the people being **oppressed.** *Yea, man," you whisper back. The other kids are already reading silently. You read a bit from his book and point to the line that says,* Except there are those who fight back. *He nods. Yea, man.*

Behind you, R Vokyea whispers excitedly to Cartisco and shows him his own open book, pointing with the length of his arm. R V is a young man that says words like cursed with a hard ed : walk ded, fight ded, kiss ded.

Part B. Based on the passage above, what is the best interpretation of the word *oppressed?*

After lunch, Decorius drags some desks apart,
metal legs squealing across the wax,
room for a 6 by 6 foot box
of empty space in front of the whiteboard.
Terrylicia's fingers tap the spacebar
as D wiggles out of his backpack,
and the deep bass plays, drummy thwacks
and melodic commands for all his body parts—

D-boy's yellow torso bends svelte,
his hands, his knees, his elbows thrusting out

and his eyes are closed, dancing to transcend,
hips flicking around, his fists and knotted belt
and navy blue legs swinging out,
his feet etching in the wax new words for his friends.

Put One Hand Up, Lean Back

Seeing you write in your journal keeps them writing.
Their elbows press the desk with each new word,
and if, like them, you lean your body toward
the page: a harmony of scribbles and scratches,
music for your teacher ears, a chorus of secret
prayers and painful thoughts in memory stored—
their blood spilling as truth and ink and words,
trophies of that fight between pen and heart.

But probably you're overthinking it. In those squeaks
of their fidgeting feet is just the latest catchy beat
of some new dance (there's always some new dance)—
the nae-naeing of minds in young romance—
and you want to dance too, be cool for once,
A few extra minutes, you say, all nonchalant.

Sway Your Body from Side to Side

Their parents 'hot breath
Swelling the walls and the bleachers
The gym all filled with sweat
And Kirk Franklin on the speakers
Singing their voices climb
Kiss the ceiling their bodies
Sway almost in time
Rows of improper copies
Elbows and shaky knees
Parodying yours and singing
Every note out of key
Their fleshy hot breath breathing
How could love ever forget
the breathing of the young?

Let Them Say Goodbye First

You enjoy the misfits the most, usually.
The boy, two years old for his grade,
smiling that wicked smile from your dreams, a tie
offered out between you like a flag of truce.
They know how to make you shout, but choose
to make you laugh instead. *Yea, I ll tie it—*
his shirt stiff and white across the shoulders.
He doesn't notice when you reach to peel the sticker
off the side—the shirt's too big, sure,
but all filled out with that youthful pride.
You give a low smile as he struts over
to the others, pink tie meeting blue
meeting green, all of them standing puffed
out like marshmallows ready for the fire.

Keep A Scrapbook

The new kid trying to be tough
With her eyes closed and her head
Tucked in her elbow, but she
Isn't asleep, you can tell,
Your back wants to tense up
When you look down at her bluff.

The class clown pinned
To the hallway wall by your angry
Barking, his fingers poking at
All the papers taped and hanging,
While your words paste him up on
The wall to hang there too.

The older girl reading
Her favorite book, with new braids
Coal-dark and twisted
On her head as if she were spun up on
A potter's wheel, the potter obsessed
With snakes, or sailor's knots.

The young man preaching to himself
In the corner, his teenage body
Growing huge, a big face too,

With a mouth two fists across
And deep brown eyes,
Fingers like gavels.

Take Attendance Data Seriously

Losing their names is something they don't say.
You forget more each week while voices low,
pitched flat as through a wall, replay:
their shouts, their jokes still purr and echo,
little bundles of noise humming at you
through the cool fogged glass of the dairy aisle
on your way to the milk. Whispers cut through
the traffic of your new commute, and all the while
the names just sneak away, a few at a time,
one or two or three holding on, some sounds
sticking in your ear like Silverstein rhymes.
The list gets so small when you put it down,
even though the noises in your head stay the same,
the laughter, the young love—just not the names.

You'll Need Therapy

You hear a faint instrumental playlist,
study music drumming down your back,
across your shoulders. You reach for your wife's hand
at the new year's party when someone quips
What is it you do? Your tongue and lips twist
over the sounds that come. You smile and stand,
your back itches, *Where s the bathroom?* You wander
down the hall, people talking of gyms and lists.

New clothes come with a price. Your body leaves
the classroom, but you still feel its big eyes
across your back, its chin side-cocked as you leave.
You laugh and you smile, but that black clip-on tie
sits fat on the closet shelf like a loaded gun—
too easy to forget the damned thing weighs a ton.

Acknowledgements

Special thanks to the following journals:

"Get Used to Shrugs" - published in *San Gabriel Valley Poetry Quarterly*

"(C) Antibodies" – published in *3 Elements Review*

"Keep a Few Dollars in Your Desk", "Keep a Few Dollars in Your Desk," "Keep One Hand Up, Lean Back," "Let Them Say Goodbye First," "Answers Their Questions as Best You Can," "You'll Need Therapy," and "Keep a Scrapbook" – published in *Fourth and Sycamore*

Joshua Roark received his MFA in poetry and works as a writing professor at Antioch University. His book of sonnets about teaching middle school as an alumnus of Teach for America was published by Unsolicited Press. In addition to his poetry, Joshua is a screenwriter and filmmaker in Los Angeles, collaborating frequently with his wife, Jo Rochelle. Their most recent project, *Dead Deer High,* premiered at the SXSW Film Festival in 2026 and is Joshua's debut screenplay.

About Dead Deer High

Created by teachers, *Dead Deer High* follows a team of high school slam poets and their English teacher as they prepare for a national poetry competition one year after a tragic shooting changed their lives forever.

The film was made by husband and wife team Jo Rochelle & Joshua Roark, who met as teachers in the Mississippi Delta.

The film World Premiered at the 2026 SXSW Film Festival.

Learn more: www.deaddeerhigh.com

Sign up for the newsletter to stay up to date on how you and others can watch the film.

All inquiries are welcome to deaddeerhigh@gmail.com, or our publicist Jason Kaspersky at jk@prodigypublicrelations.com.

www.ingramcontent.com/pod-product-compliance
Lightning Source LLC
Chambersburg PA
CBHW021348060726
47591CB00006B/2223